Conquering The EneME!

Conquering The EneME!

Being delivered from self and self-imposed limitations

Annette Jones-Ward, M.A.

AuthorHouse™
1663 Liberty Drive
Bloomington, IN 47403
www.authorhouse.com
Phone: 1-800-839-8640

Published by AuthorHouse 06/04/2012

ISBN: 978-1-4772-1645-3 (sc)
ISBN: 978-1-4772-1644-6 (hc)
ISBN: 978-1-4772-1643-9 (e)

Library of Congress Control Number: 2012910212

This book is printed on acid-free paper.

Contents

Acknowledgements

I'D FIRST LIKE to thank God for without him nothing in my life is or was ever possible but with him I have been able to and can do all things. Second I'd like to thank God for purposing in my heart to write this book because it's something I never envisioned prior to 3 years ago yet as I began to write and put the book in one direction, God caused me to lose the original copy and begin again in another direction . . . . showing me yet again my life is not my own and that I have no control over the direction my life is going. God I thank you for choosing me and being patient enough with me thru my disobedience, slougherness and sometimes unwillingness to do what you called me to do. God for every mountain you've brought me over, for every trial you've seen me through, for every blessing hallelujah . . . . for this and in all things I give you all the praise.

To the best thing next to the holy trinity in my life—God's gift (after Jesus) to me—my mother (and father) Ms. Ethelyn Jones. Mom, although I love words both big and small, words can never express how much I love you!! I don't really know what direction my life would've taken had you not been there every step of the way as a mother and a father. I thank you for being a mother when I needed, a father that provided, a friend when I needed a shoulder and an ear, a wonderful grandmother to my kids, a surrogate mother to my friends when they needed you . . . thank you for being you and I love you for always being there and never giving up on me. I love you with everything in me . . . . man God couldn't have given me a better mom . . . . he did that!!!

To my kids Darriane (Dee) and Troy Jr.(T.J) . . . . you all are the gifts after Jesus and right before Grandma ☺ I love the two of you and all my hard work is because of you all. I thank the two of you for being the driving force in my life. You don't know how much the two of you motivate me and I love you for being patient with me when I have to work endless hours to accomplish all that God has ordained for me to do. Also to my babies Reginald Jr., Reginae and Ryanna, I Love You all now and forever.

To my sweetie, my heart, love of my life, my first love that has returned to be my last love . . . the man God created for me, my husband and friend Reginald Ward, Sr. I thank you for your support and for loving me when I wasn't always lovely. You encourage me, support me, stand with me, go before me, protect and provide for me and our kids . . . . all that a man is supposed to do and for this I love you!!!

To my family—brothers Rodney and Terry, sisters Schanell, Sharon and Debra, my favorite Aunt Marion, Favorite Cousins Antoinette, Kendra, my godkids Felicia Gaudin, Larry Francois III and Riya Batiste, my son/nephew Jermain Abdin, other aunts, uncles, cousins, brothers, sisters, nieces, nephews, great nieces and nephews, great-great nieces and the Ward Family (that loved me from the beginning and has shown me love even when I didn't know it:) . . . I love you all very much and not just because you're my family, but also because you're a blessing to my life. Lastly, R.I.P to my Guardian Angel Uncle Sammy who stepped in and acted as my dad when he knew I didn't have one. If love could've held you here, you would still be here with me however I loved you but God loved you best . . . . indeed God got an angel when he got you.

To my church family, “The City of Love”, especially the music ministry which I am a part of . . . you all have shown me so much love since I became a part of this family, it’s almost as if I’ve always been here . . . . I love you all!!! Most importantly to Bishop Lester and Pastor Fran Love, I’ve never seen anything like I’ve seen at TCOL, the love is so real and your concern for the lives of your people is so genuine and sincere. Before connecting with this ministry, I knew somewhat of who I was in God however, could never leap in faith and just walk in it. After joining The City of Love, I not only felt I could walk in faith, but like the eagle I felt I could fly. Your ministry has connected me to God in such a way that I could have never imagined, has helped me to trust God like never before and be able to give myself away. I now realize the life I live is not for my benefit but for God’s glory and to be ok with knowing I am nothing but with him I can do all things. Bishop and Pastor Fran you have been such a driving force in my life and I personally want to say thank you and I love the both of you, so Devil eat your heart out (thanks Pastor Fran for letting me borrow that)!!

To my best friends in the whole entire world, Lakara Foster, Chrishanda Robinson, Donnis Brown, good friends Felicia Simmons, Angelique Francois, Shantel Pajeaud, Ayanna Toney, Dominique Moore and life time friend since kindergarten Natasha Charles (and my accountant—thank God for lifelong friends . . . . man yall have been there for it all from Nette from the project to the me that stands before you today . . . the old and newly converted me . . . . man thank you for accepting me flaws and all. Don't know what would've happened if I didn't have some of yalls shoulders to cry on and ears to talk into. We have laughed, cried, fought, fell out . . . BUT WE STILL TOGETHER and I thank God for you!!

Last but certainly no least I dare not close this dedication out without giving special acknowledgments to those who have truly motivated me and are partly responsible for my success. I'd like to say a special thanks to those that some refer to as "haters" but I'd like to refer to them as "my helpers" for you have motivated me to speak less and kneel more, to sleep less and pray more, to not accept less but seek God for all the more . . . . you've caused me crazy problems which in turn has brought forth crazy praise . . . . You've forced me to seek God like never before which in turn has caused me to do things I never thought possible . . . . you have pushed me into purpose so for this I owe you a thanks.

His word says eyes have not seen nor ears heard nor has entered into the heart of men what God has in store for me . . . . So with that being said, keep talking and naysaying but also keep watching . . . God's doing a BIG thing in me . . . . eat your heart out!!! #Chucking up the Deuces!!

INTRODUCTION

THE REASON I wrote this book is to tell the truth, the whole truth and nothing but the truth in order to help others recognize what and who in several cases is our biggest dream snatcher and the enemy that hinders progression into purpose . . . . self!! In helping others to recognize the voice of the inner enemy, it is my prayer that you have the same ah-ha experience I did. I will tell you my story, not for the sake of just telling you my business but so that you can recognize the patterns in your life as you encounter it and so that you are equipped to conquer your eneME each time he/she arises. I'll share all of my fears, insecurities and short-comings hoping to save someone from making the mistakes I did and to prohibit someone else from wasting as much time as I have on the way to purpose. This is no longer the season to allow opportunities to pass us by because of our own self-imposed limitations and other self-sabotaging behaviors. It's time that we bury all the I Can'ts, What ifs and If I do and move from promise to purpose.

I've seen self-sabotage on so many levels in myself and have begun to see it in the lives of young ladies I've been mentoring over the years however I share my experience with them in hopes of breaking the vicious cycle. I've known the crippling power of fear and the power of the little voice that speaks to us convincing us that we will fail before we even make an attempt to succeed. Fear is something that we will have with us always and quite often there are times when fear serves a good cause like when we're walking down a dark alley it prompts us to move swiftly in order to avoid danger. It's only when we make life altering decisions based on fear that prohibit our ability to move, progress and ultimately live, supporting rationale for failing (e.g. I can't finish school, I will never be in a loving relationship, etc.) is fear counter-productive. My intentions are not to lie to you and tell you once you read this book you will never have fear again and you'll be able to solve all your problems right away. That would be a lie because there are times I still encounter fear but the purpose is to assist you with identifying the enemy as it arises (in writing the book I had situations and recognized the enemy arising almost immediately), your potential and true purpose in life, to assist you with taking steps into the purpose God has ordained for your life and overall with conquering the eneME in order to succeed in life. I am now more aware of my fears and am able to address fear based thinking and behaviors a lot sooner so that they're not destroying my destiny.

Learning to counter the attacks of your eneME will assist you with overcoming and managing fear in your life. It's a very normal emotion which you will have encounters with all your life especially when being made to step outside of your comfort zone, however if properly managed fear does not have to prohibit progression into your true purpose. I indeed understand far too well the set of difficulties life tends to project at us which is why I dedicate this book to my ladies (although men are welcomed to read it) of all ages, 5-105 because I saw first-hand the struggles of my mom raising my brother and I as a single parent, I know what it's like to be neglected by my dad someone you know should love you and you did nothing for them not to, to look for love in the wrong places, to be a fool for love, to live beyond a bad relationship after a bad relationship after yet another bad relationship, to survive a divorce, to be a single mother, to be a single mother/woman in a marriage, not have much support, to endure impoverished situations—to walk a mile in the shoes of a woman because I have been it all. This book will make you think, make you move, make you grow, make you flourish and make you know your own strength and realize that if you get outta your own way, you too can win. I'm prepared to share the good bad and ugly to assure that the readers of this book will begin to practice self-encouragement and omit self-sabotage, be your own star player.

Chapter 1

What is an EneMe??

But I say unto you, Love your enemies, bless them that curse you, do good to them that hate you and pray for them which despitefully use you and persecute you . . . Matthew 5:44

WHEN SOLDIERS GO to war, the ultimate goal is to come out victorious. As they plan their attack, troops must strategize on how to attack and ultimately conquer the enemy. This strategic planning process includes thinking ahead and also delving into the mind of the enemy, contemplating how they will come, what they may or may not do, what weapons may be used, etc. Ultimately, this entire war and victory is mapped out in their minds first before any attempts are made to fight the battle. The enemy strategizes in the same manner because his desire is to win as well. If he can kill the will of the opponent to fight by overpowering and/or instilling enough fear into the opponent, the battle is won before it starts. Relating this action to something more applicable in our time, in the sport of boxing, Muhammad Ali honed the phrase "float like a butterfly sting like a bee" when referencing his style of fighting. He used this phrase as an intimidation tactic on his opponents to let them know that he moves so fast they won't be able to land a hit but his hit is that of a bee sting, one most memorable. Ali often referred to himself as "The Greatest" and used his pre-match time to "trash talk" to his opponents often times in rhymes. This trash talk was a way to kill his enemy's will or instill enough fear into his opponent they'd lose the desire to fight him. His speech was so persuasive, he convinced some of his opponents that he could not be beat. On many occasions this worked in Ali's favor and has granted him a place in history as one of the Greatest Boxers of our time. As for Ali, he often times defeated his enemies in their minds with what he said before the match began, simply because he'd convinced them that he was a champion and they were not. Therefore the victory occurred prior to the beginning of the fight. The motive of the enemy is the same. He uses our own "little voice" to talk enough trash to us and instills enough fear to cripple us so that we are not walking into our life's purpose and zap us of their will to fight but who or what is that "little voice" that trash talks us?

Is that spelled right??

For the purpose in which I'm speaking of EneMe, the spelling is absolutely right. How many times have you heard what you refer to as the little voice in the back of your head whisper in your ear, "You can't do that", "You're not worthy of this" or "What if you mess up when you try to . . ." and after that convince yourself that the lies are in some way true. Better yet, how many times have you talked yourself out of opportunities that have been presented to you by saying "Oh, I'm not smart enough to do that" or "I don't have enough money to accomplish that" or "No one in my family ever succeeded doing this so let me stop fooling myself." You officially zap yourself of a desire to fight by means of self-sabotage being your biggest critic and your own worst enemy!! You are now the person that decides you're inadequate which means you settle for mediocrity, possesses a narrow or no view of success and are hesitant with progress, the one killing your own will to progress into purpose—a practicing self-abuser. This is something I've not only seen in others but myself on more occasions than I care to mention. We've become immune to greatness figuring it's only a figment of our imagination. So much so that we no longer strive for success as a result of either fear of failure, some form of inadequacies, adopting a spirit of procrastination or merely narrowing our views to accommodate our narrow manners of thinking . . . if I strive for small things there's no way I can fail because the big is out of my reach. I know my spirit is saying to start my own business but I don't think I'll be successful so, I'll get this job instead of opening my own business. This means we've overlooked God, our faith and ultimately our purpose and minimized our very existence. We've not only boxed ourselves in but we've minimized a Big Omnipresent God to our size. Silly us!!! That makes me ponder on the term enemy and what and how we differentiate between the enemy and the eneME?? Anybody that has taken any type of science class past elementary school, has taken some form of Biology course anatomy and knows that lots of dissection takes place regarding the anatomy. We study the anatomy of people, animals etc. to understand their structure, position or overall function—what makes them tick in other words. So what juices your enemy/eneME? What's their position or purpose in your life? But first we need to identify who they are.

Webster gives us a clear definition of what an enemy is. Mr. Webster defines an enemy as one who is antagonistic to another; especially one seeking to injure, overthrow or confound an opponent. We know all too well how to identify most enemies or what we so commonly refer to as haters today because they are those that oppose us, talk against and about us, those that try killing our reputations or even those that are actually trying to kill us physically. I know if you just read the scripture where Jesus commands us to love our enemies, the one that opposes us, hates us and desires to kill us, you may be saying "yeah that's easier said than done" or "yeah that may be easy for Jesus but I ain't him"!!! Whatever the case may be, we all know that we have enemies and it's a difficult task to love someone that you know beyond the shadow of a doubt does not like you, may even hate you, will use you and depending on the intensity of the hate will kill you. It actual takes us to look at these identified people not as haters but as helpers because they actually help to push you to your destiny. They said "oh she ain't gon be nothing" and in your mind you counter that by saying "I'm gon show her" and you actually succeed. Without that extra push and your attempt to counter what the external enemy has said (or as you said "to show her") you may have not have been as successful so in all actuality that person's negative words and they're hating on you has helped you. That's the enemy that we can recognize right away but what about the little subtle voice that speaks defeat to us yet we don't recognize its malicious intents to kill our destiny nor do we attempt to "show her" but we believe them . . . your true enemy!! Whoa but Webster neglected to define the EneME??? What or Who is it???

WHO??????????? . . . . ME!!

With an identified enemy we can ask . . . Jesus are you serious?? Do you really want me to love the very individual whose entire existence is spent on seeing me not exist? How do you suppose I do something like that? Better than that even if I don't hate them as they do me, I sure don't want to pray for them because they mean me no good so why should I? These questions are easy to ask and we resist all that God says regarding the enemy when we think in terms of the enemy being an external person. Has God shown you a vision and you still have not attempted to make it a reality? Is there a house you really want to buy but you tell yourself I will never have the money to get it and you dismiss the thought before you even try? You know that you have the skills, the knowledge and all it takes to start a business but your fear outweigh your faith and therefore your business remains a thought and a dream? Have you ever minimized your abilities (e.g. need to lose weight yet keep eating all the wrong things while telling yourself . . . . Somebody has to be my size)? Ok neither of those were your area, then let me try something else. Your dream is to finish school, but your little voice says you're too old, you don't have the money and you just ultimately tell God No not right now maybe at a time when I'm straight. Yeah you are talking to the God that owns all the cattle on a thousand hills, the earth and everything in it with the full capability of getting you straight!!

Guilty, Guilty, and Guilty. I know one time it was so funny God put something in my spirit to do which was going to be the biggest leap of faith I'd ever taken. First I thought it was a case of mistaken identity and that he'd confused me with someone else. When the word came back to my spirit, I needed confirmation. A week later my Bishop confirmed it in his sermon but I had to go to God one more time. Man I was tryna get outta that thang I had gone as far as to tell myself God didn't mean that and told God you know my responsibilities I can't do that. Later in the book I will share what this incident was. I am sharing my times but how many times have you talked yourself out of opportunities that you felt you couldn't achieve before making an attempt? How many times have you used the excuse of not having support, family, etc. is why you can't succeed, or the time you said, it's too hard to do . . . So you just forget it and do something easier. What if the person that tells you the most negative stuff, kills your chances at opportunity before it can get started, tell you what you can't do before you even make an effort is in fact not external but internal? The person that stares back at you when you look in the mirror—the eneME (now do you see why I spelled it wrong . . . lol)????

Much of my life, I didn't believe I was able to do much of what God had spoken to my spirit to do for several reasons either because I didn't have the money to do so, because I didn't feel I had enough intellect to do so, because I'd never seen an example of it done in my family, feelings of inferiority because of my upbringings in a nutshell FEAR. I allowed myself to be crippled by fear and no matter how much God had allowed me to accomplish, I was still plagued with a sense of inferiority still in the mindset of being lil ol' Nette from the Project. Fear caused me to suffer from an identity crisis not realizing who God called me to be and therefore not walking in the purpose he'd ordained for my life. I had to learn not to see myself thru my eyes but to see me as God does and no matter what it looked like or how intimidating the tasks seemed, to believe that I could do all things thru and with Christ except fail. Simply put, God promised to do exceeding abundantly above all we can ask or think which means if I could think it, then it's too small he's doing bigger things then that and that whatever it is . . . “It’s a new thing” and that I could no longer be responsible for my own demise. That in order to avoid failure and to succeed I had to learn to Conquer the EneMe!!!

CHAPTER 2

Hushhh, Hushhh!!

And do not be conformed to this world, but be transformed by the renewal or your mind, that by testing you may discern what is the will of God, what is good and acceptable and perfect. Romans 12:2

SILENCING THE ENEME!!

As a profession, I chose to be or rather my calling is to be a Mental Health Counselor. I was always intrigued by the workings on the human mind and infatuated with the idea of being able to understand people, what makes them tick, how the brain works and ultimately how the working or non-working of the mind dictates behavior. In addition to that people have always felt way too comfortable telling me their personal business, and I enjoy helping others to work thru their problems. I can recall when I worked as a Program Manager for a Mental Health Rehab agency, one day I had a case to come across my desk where a mom was seeking help for her daughter to get treatment. The daughter was exhibiting extreme behaviors where she'd snap in class, throw chairs, hit teachers and students, use profanity, etc. When asked the reason for her behavior she'd say the voice of the little boy in her head told her to do it. After reporting the behaviors and the report of the auditory commands of the "little boy in her head" to our Psychiatrist, he diagnosed the little girl with a Mental Disorder called Schizophrenia. Schizophrenia is characterized by a breakdown of thought processes and poor emotional responsiveness whereas in most cases manifests itself in auditory hallucinations (hearing voices of people not present), paranoia and delusions. Those suffering from this disorder, often time find themselves chronically unemployed, living in poverty and sometimes homeless but the most they'll report is the voices they hear in their heads. In order to silence the voices, those suffering with this disorder must take antipsychotic medications (Clozapine, Risperdal, etc.). The medication is used to regulate behaviors and ultimately silence the voices that are negatively dictating to these individuals. Therefore if there's a way to silence the voices that speak negatively to those suffering from Schizophrenia, there are definitely ways for us to silence the voices of the eneME that speaks negatively to us however it's not thru medication but strategies.

Researchers have found that 78% of our self-talk is negative which means only 22% of the time we're spending time boosting ourselves as opposed to criticizing, doubting or sabotaging ourselves. The first step is to silencing the eneMe is to recognize his/her language which most of the statements start with: "I can't", "I shouldn't", "Yeah, but" and the most famous "What If"? So how do we Silence the EneME?? We'll discuss three approaches I use when I have a decision to make, when fears creep in and the eneMe begins to rise(in addition to praying) 1. I find a cure to the “what if” syndrome 2. Put Mind over matter and 3. I expose the negatives (talks, thoughts and behaviors) and replace them.

THE WHAT IF SYNDROME

The fortunate thing about fear is that 90% of the things that we fear or worry about never come true which means of all of the "What if" scenarios we create, only 10% of these scenarios will come to pass. The What if syndrome? This is not an actual illness or syndrome is what I assume you're saying however let me show you how it is. Any medical or psychological illness that's labeled a syndrome is characterized by symptoms, behaviors or characteristics that point to a particular disorder or condition. Symptoms of "what if" are based on many forms of one symptom. One that cripples and handicaps progression into purpose, results in failure and an inability to live a productive life or the life God has designed for us . . . Fear!! It looks or sounds like this: What if my business fails? What if I lose my house trying to start my own business? What if I don't like the career and spend all these years in school? What if I get in the plane and it crashes? What if I buy the home and lose my job and can't pay for it? What if . . . what if . . . what if . . . ??? Have you ever noticed that most of our "what ifs" have negative connotations? Well like my mom used to tell me (as many have said) "If "IF" was a 5th we'd all be drunk which means if we'd drink as many fifths of alcoholic beverages in comparison to the amount of ifs we have then we'd be consistently drunk. FEAR is merely False Expectations Appearing Real and we have complete control of it, we can address it and in many cases discover a cure to this problem.

Why is it that we often times have so many ifs, most of which are negative. Quite often the ifs are triggered by fear, self-doubt and it leads us to talk ourselves out of opportunities instead of into them. These "what ifs" are closely associated with a lack of trust in our own abilities and us yielding to the voice of the eneME that is guilty of being our inner dream snatcher. Ultimately our "what if" questions causes us the make plans to fail as opposed to planning to succeed, "if I quit my job to start my business and the business fails then I won't have any money and won't be able to pay my house note, and I'll lose my car and be hungry cause I won't be able to buy food then I'll live under the bridge and I don't want all that to happen" and quite often it's rambled just like that. The more we say the more scenarios we come up with the bigger the snowball of doubt gets. At that rate we've developed our failure plan and we stay in what appears to be our comfort zone. I'll stay on this job at least I know I'll get paid every 2 weeks and can pay for my house, etc. You bailed on what could have been a great opportunity and even your purpose in life on the false pretense of the comfort, you become complacent, stuck!! Well if I can infuse some reality, there is no guarantee that the boss there will keep you on and if that be the case then you'll be fired and not collecting a check every 2 weeks—comfort zone no longer comfortable!! The one thing I learned about life is the only thing that is consistent is CHANGE whether you're prepared or not . . . it will happen!!

Fear of the unknown triggers our "what ifs" and are based on a probability and not a reality. Our fears are usually not evidence based yet they instill enough fear to consume us and increase our level of anxiety. Just enough to handicap or cripple us and hinder our ability to walk into the purpose that's been set for our lives. Just what if we changed the tone of our questioning to positive "what ifs"? What if taking the leap of faith leads me to endless opportunities? What if I enjoy being self-employed and make so much money I can pay my house out years ahead of time? What if my business does so well that I have 3 locations in the next 2 years? What if I enjoy flying so much, I decide to travel more and have the opportunity to see more of the world that I've ever thought of? We can all agree that what we say motivates how we think and that positive self-talk and thinking has greater benefits than the negatives.

Mind Over Matter

Mind over Matter was a very popular phrase in the 1960's and 70's which was originally used to make reference to paranormal activities. It's when an individual possesses the ability to use the activity of the mind to move items and ultimately demonstrate the power the mind possesses. It has also been used in the spiritual realm to make reference to the link between an individuals' thoughts and how thoughts manipulate what we say and our behaviors which determines success or failure in life. We have Bible verses that says "So a man thinks, so is he or the aforementioned scripture that tells us transformation takes place with the renewing of our minds which says when we change how we think, it'll change what we say/believe, how we behave and ultimately change the sequence of events in one's life. The beginning of changing negatives is to replace it with positives and silencing the voices that are speaking negatively to us even when it is self. It's one's perception that will help with allowing a positive mindset to rule over a situation, no matter what it is. I guess you can call it "the choosing to look at the glass as half full as opposed to half empty" effect.

Quite often our fears motivate what we say and how we think but as the Bible speaks of the renewing of one's mind initiates a change in behavior. We lack the necessary confidence in self to accomplish many of the goals we're destined to accomplish. If God has given us the vision to accomplish a goal then therefore he'll make the provisions. He doesn't call the qualified, he qualifies the called. I know with my personal experience, God purposed me to start a non-profit organization, which meant developing a curriculum, running the business, writing grants, being my own employee and so much more. All of which I'd never done before and didn't have any examples of it in my family. For some time I'd said to myself "I don't know anything about running a business", "I can't grow this business", "I don't know anything about being a boss", "What if I mess this all up"? "What if the business flops"? I was scared, uncertain, overwhelmed, anxious . . . everything negative nothing positive. It was so bad, that when I began to get people soliciting the services, I became extremely fearful feeling I couldn't do it all on my own and just shut down. It took me about a year to resume services and for me to place my membership at a new church until I began to see myself as God sees me. One that is able to do all things thru Christ except fail. That's not to say that there are not still times I question myself and the "what ifs" jump in but it doesn't take me long to recognize the negative and transition my questions into positive what ifs. This therefore allows me to talk myself into opportunities instead of out of them besides nothing beats a failure but a try.

Exposing The Negatives

In Photography I can remember when we would take our 110 film to the store to have the pictures that we'd taken developed. We'd go and pick our pictures up from wherever they were developed and in the package were the pictures and the negatives. In learning a little something about photography (and I mean a little), when the negatives are exposed to the proper amount of lighting they will reproduce bright portions of the photographed subject and create images. This image from the negative is then transferred onto paper which in turn produces a positive photographic print. A negative used to create a positive, I thought wow how profound is that?? If we take our negatives, expose them and project them onto paper we can create positive pictures of our lives. How much more effective is that if we apply it to our daily lives. What would happen if I project all of my negatives (thoughts, sayings, etc.) onto paper? Would that allow me to be able to convert them into positives? (ex. left side of paper: I'll lose weight, my whole family is fat!! . . . right side of paper: If I make small changes in my diet daily and exercise more I can gradually lose weight.). If I write the vision and make it plain, will that surely allow my purpose and vision to come to pass?

My non-profit organization has an all-girls program in which we teach social, life and entrepreneurship skills along with teaching girls, etiquette, building self-esteem and all skills needed to assist the girls with making successful transitions into womanhood. One of our first activities is called an "I Can't" Funeral. The purpose of the funeral is so that the girls can bury everything negative they've ever been told by someone else or by themselves that they can't do. From here they proceed through the program knowing that they can do all things thru Christ because he strengthens them. This activity is followed by creation of vision boards so after burying the "I can'ts" and following up with visions of what they want to accomplish in life, they're able to change their way of thinking and what they say as it regards self and accomplishments. Knowing that all things are possible therefore nothing is impossible, this allows them to be able to do things they've never thought possible like going to college, starting a business, being a first generation college graduate. For the reenacted funeral, we have an actual program and a make-shift coffin (a decorated shoe box). Members are given pieces of paper to write the negative statements onto. EXAMPLES: “I can’t lose weight” “I can’t be a Dr. when I grow up” “I can’t dance/sing” They’re allowed 5-10 minutes to think and write. Members who wish can share what they write but only voluntarily and they’re then instructed to fold the papers in half and bring them to the front. Have them place their “I Can’t” statements into the make shift coffin and after everyone has placed their I Can’ts in the coffin the lid is placed on the box. This is the act of burying their “I Can’ts”! The Leader then delivers the eulogy:

> ***“Friends, we’re gathered here today to honor the memory of ‘I Can’t.’ While he was with us here on earth, he touched the lives of everyone, some more than others. We have provided ‘I Can’t’ with a final resting place and a headstone that contains his epitaph. He is survived by his brothers and sisters, ‘I Can’, ‘I Will’, and ‘I’m Going to Right Away’. Though they may not be as popular as their famous relative and certainly not as strong and powerful yet, perhaps someday, with your help, they will make an even bigger mark on the world. May ‘I Can’t’ rest in peace and may everyone present pick up their lives and move forward in his absence . . .”***

As part of the celebration, a large tombstone can be made with the words “I Can’t” at the top, RIP in the middle and the date added at the bottom. The paper tombstone can hang in meeting every week as a reminder.

Once the negative thoughts are replaced with positive thoughts and self-talk, then positive behaviors begin to manifest. So as opposed to the message “I can’t do it”, you’re saying “If I plan properly, I can accomplish this”, you’re replacing the statement “I’m not good enough to receive this” with “I am fearfully and wonderfully made and that the favor of God is following me”!! Thru positive affirmations you begin to see yourself differently, do things differently, reach for goals, begin to dream again and therefore are able to accomplish your goals and live the life that you’ve been pre-ordained to live.

CHAPTER 3

Note To Self

How precious to me are your thoughts, O God! How vast is the sum of them! If I would count them, they are more than the sand, I awake and I am still with you! Psalm 139:17-18

IN THE PREVIOUS chapters we begin to recognize the trends or patterns of our often self-defeating behaviors and how far too often we sabotage our own opportunities to succeed. When we begin to accept responsibility for our own successes and failures in life, we regain our power and authority. We can then and only then begin to see true progression in our lives. Many of us have traversed a life polluted by drug and/or sexual abuse, neglect and/or abandonment and can use all of these mishaps as justification for failure. However instead of being angry, bitter or miserable, we should appreciate life's trials and allow them to mold us into being productive and optimistic people. Successful people are those that can grow against all odds, yet can keep their dreams alive while refusing to conform to societal norms. One is not defeated when the world says you will fail, you are only defeated when you begin to internalize the external negatives and convince yourself that the naysayers are correct. You ask what does all that mean?? Simply put, if the world says (as it has) that since you are the kid of a single parent, you will fail academically and therefore will remain in poverty throughout your life span, that's one thing . . . not really the truth but that's what "they" say. It's not until you convince yourself of this untruth, that you will fail academically and be poor for your entire lifespan. The Bible's teachings are that life and death are in the power of the tongue. If you say, "I can do all things thru Christ . . ." then you will be able to do all things. If you say to self, "I will have more than I can ask or think . . ." then that's what you will have. Just as if you say "My family never succeeded so I'm bound to be a failure" then indeed you'll be a failure. It's all in whose report you believe. So make this a note to self: watch your mouth because what you say is what you get!!!

You Are What You Say

Words are very powerful and are used to speak life and death both physically and rhetorically. The Bible teaches us that life and death are in the power of the tongue and therefore what we say determines our level of success or failure. God demonstrates the power of speaking when he chose to speak the Heavens and the Earth into existence. He said, "Let there be light" and there was. God not only spoke the world into existence but he spoke us into existence as well and is still speaking to us today. Unfortunately quite often because of the sinful flesh, we stop listening, we tune God out, give room to disobedience, and fall off the path that God has set for us. He says "we can do all things but fail" yet we say oh that's too hard I can't do that. Often times it's what we say that causes the demise of our dreams, goals and ultimate path to living the good life. Far too often our speech is motivated by a fear, be it a fear of failure, succeeding, fear of being in a relationship, falling in love, etc. We say things like, If I succeed and make a lot of money, my friends will think I'm too much, If I fall in love with him, I stand the chance of getting hurt or If I get this job, I might not be able to perform on it. With this form of self-sabotaging communication and desire to not be disliked, hurt or isolated, we talk ourselves out of opportunities. What we say coincides with how we think which in turn dictates how we act. It's ultimately what we do or don't do determines our success or failure in life. In the aforementioned scenarios, we don't attempt to get the job, we don't fall in love and at the end of our lives we've merely existed and coasted thru life and not lived.

Self-esteem/self-confidence building is a large component of our curriculum and what we do when working with youth because of the negative effects of low self-esteem. With one of our activities, we encourage the youth to use positive affirmations in order to build positive self-esteem. Positive affirmations are merely positive statements about self. We teach how to take what was once a negative statement and converting it into a positive and the effects of the conversion. Negative statement such as "I'm fat and I'll never lose weight". On a negative note, such a statement would lead the person to believe they'll always be fat so instead of working to get the weight off, the person continues to eat unhealthy, and in the end does not lose weight. Whereas the same person that is overweight and she/he says "I'm overweight, but I have to lose this weight to live a productive life." That person figures steps to losing the weight successfully, changes their diet, exercises consistently and in the end loses the weight and has dodged the high blood pressure, diabetes bullet. The path to success for one and failure for the other began with something the individual said—The Power of Words.

Thought Provoking Sayings

Fortunately we can change our thoughts and behavior with words. Examples of positive affirming statements would go something like this: "I have the power to change my situation", "I am good at what I do", "I love and accept myself". It's time we begin to encourage ourselves by accentuating our positives and eliminating our negatives. What we say ultimately dictates how we think and how we behave. In other words what we say determines our success and/or failure. We must no longer allow ourselves to be victims to our fears, past failures, thoughts and negative desires. Unfortunately, we are victims to our own minds and way of thinking and at times we have to speak positive and simply encourage ourselves even when our thoughts or circumstances are the total opposite!! It's time that we eliminate excuses (which I learned from a meeting I attended are tools of incompetence which build monuments of nothing=excuses) and become ok with succeeding. We must walk into the purpose and the destiny God has ordained for us excluding the hindrances that prohibit us from doing so especially when it's something as minute as changing our vocabulary.

God has given us all talents and a purpose, however if we excuse ourselves from it all and walk in fear then we can never walk into our purpose and fulfill God's plan for our lives. Is this an easy process . . . . I don't know how else to say this "HELL NO" however the rewards outweigh the struggles. There's a poem written by an anonymous author I read that speaks of the road to success. It paints the picture that this road is not the shortest distance between 2 points as we learned in school is a straight line. Success is actually accomplished upon traveling a road filled with many obstacles. The poem tells us that there are curves called Failure, loops called Confusion, Speed bumps called Friends, Red lights that attempt to stop your progression called Enemies, Caution lights called Family and flats that hinder our progression called Jobs(especially those that are not our passion and in some cases hate but stay to collect a paycheck). The writer, after painting a picture of what can deter us on our way to success, he then begins to inspire by telling us that if we have a spare called Determination, an engine called Perseverance (that allows us to keep pushing), Insurance (and assurance) called Faith and a driver called God then surely we will arrive safely to our intended destination which is a place called Success.

Changing your perception

If we do an evaluation of successful people, we can determine that on the road to success there has indeed been some hesitation, some fear, some narrow views and the overcoming of obstacles to get to the point of success. The only difference between those that have become victim to the ene-ME and those that succeed, it is that the successful people are better able to overcome obstacles, they've learned to challenge the voice of the eneME and they also know that with every failure there is a lesson. Sometimes it takes looking at things from a different perspective, not that losing is losing but that losing is actually winning especially when a valuable lesson is learned. Successful people are optimistic, able to look at the glass as half full as opposed to half empty. An example of such, I'll share was my first marriage. This was not the best relationship which is why it ended in divorce. He was a nice guy, but it takes more than that to be a good husband. We had more than fair share of differences and in my attempt to make a long story short instead of going thru life miserable, I chose to divorce him and move on. To fast forward about a year after I divorced him, I had a friend to endure the same ordeal where she was too miserable in her marriage and wanted to divorce. She complained about it being the worst decision she'd ever made to get married and that she never wanted to get married again. You know the norm when you're in a situation like that (which was the same thing I said when I decided I wanted a divorce). I then told my friend that I wouldn't change a thing about my past because being married though was a bad experience with that person was one of my greatest learning experiences. After being shocked by my response, she later said "I'd never heard that before" and asked what did I mean. I shared with her that I learned a lot about myself, what I could tolerate in a relationship, what it means to be a good and bad wife, it revealed that I still had trust issues with men and that I'd never truly addressed a deeply rooted problem that I'd had for almost 30 years as a result of not having a relationship with my dad. I discovered that I still somewhat hated my dad and therefore would never be able to truly trust or love a man until I could overcome that. I truly learned a lot but had I not gone thru the marriage and divorce, none of this would have ever been revealed to me. So therefore, I chose to look at that experience as a learning experience as opposed to a major mistake, though I loss time, some happiness, etc. I gained so much more. It made it easier to go thru it and move past it!!! It's all in how you look at things.

Do you believe man or God who is your creator? Man says one thing but God says I shall have what I ask, that I am more than a conqueror and that I am capable of doing all things if I only believe. I think I'm going to believe the maker of every good and perfect gift, the only that parted the large body of water to save his people from evil Pharoah, the one that fed the 5000 with 2 little fish and 5 loaves of bread and yes that one that had power to lay down his life and pick it right back up as he said he would 3 days later . . . something about that Jesus . . . Note to self (myself and yourself) . . . Choose your words wisely, speak life even in what appears to be a dead situation all as you let his word do the work in your life!!!

CHAPTER 4

Discovering the Me God Sees

For you formed my inward parts; you covered me in my mother's womb. I will praise you, for I am fearfully and wonderfully made! Psalm 139: 13-14

FAR TOO OFTEN we confuse our roles and places in life and conform to that which is natural, forgetting that we are spiritual and not natural beings. We become confined and limited by the flesh in which we dwell which causes us to limit our thinking and spiritual existence. God's word says that eyes have not seen nor ears heard nor has entered into the hearts of man that which he has in store for those that love him, yet we trust in our own words about our lives which often contradicts what God says about us. We neglect to walk in purpose due to limited thoughts, fear of failure, counterproductive behaviors, fear of success, etc. In short, what we say about self often time causes us to be incapable of seeing ourselves as God sees us which in a nutshell causes us to suffer with an identity crisis never discovering who we are.

My Identity

Who are you? Who am I? Most people when asked this question will answer this question by saying their name . . . My name is . . . but what's in a name? Name is defined as a word or phrase that constitutes the distinctive designation of a person or thing. We all know especially mothers that when we deliver a baby we have to give them a name which throughout life is how they're identified. Sometimes we give them names borrowed from things, after other people or indicative of what we anticipate them being. My birth given name although I like it and have no plans to change it, is not an indicator of my life or a reflection of who I am. It labels me, not identifies me. Knowing your name is one thing, knowing your identity and who you are is something different. Far too often we assume our names identify us and we go thru life suffering with an identity crisis because we don't learn our true identity or we in some sad cases assume the wrong identity. You are from a family of lawyers so you automatically assume that's the road you should be on. In the end you discover, you totally hate law but hey your family is happy because you kept the family tradition . . . . wrong identity. I've had to overcome several struggles and was only able to attain success against odds and many difficulties and success never came easy for me. Therefore if you want a name or word that distinctively designates or indicates who I am, I have several for you to pick from but I'll settle for . . . . VICTORIOUS!!!

One that declares they are victorious has obviously encountered some form of struggle or conflict and came out a winner or on top. This is in line with God's word when he declares that we his children are more than conquerors. This sends the message that in all things we win because with God we can do all things except fail. Victory in itself is bitter sweet because although you've come out a winner, you've endured a process to get to a victorious ending which means someone had to lose or you had to lose some things. This process can be in man on man combat which is physical or between your spirit and mind which is mental and internal. When your spirit tells you that you can do all things thru Christ because he strengthens you and yet your mind says well you don't have the education, money or know how to do this. Your battle is in your mind, an internal struggle with your eneME!!

In the heat of battle is when you encounter the struggles, sweat, pain and tears. As a Christian we understand that the battle is not ours to win but that we must show up prepared for it. The Bible declares in II Chronicles 20:15 that the battle is not ours it's the Lord's which means it's impossible for us to lose and that the battle is won before we get there to fight it but it still means we must show up. This is where we get to encounter another facet of God and know him as Jehovah Nissi—our Banner, our victory because he alone is the one who wins our battle and therefore in him we are victorious. This is the same as the battles we fight inwardly. Our spirit must show up prepared for battle against flesh. The spirit is the real you and what connects with God and if you show up with God, the spirit wins. It is what gets us to see beyond physical limitations and achieve what seems impossible. The spirit knows that there are no limits and no boundaries to what we are capable of doing because it recognizes your God given potential. So what steps can be taken to allow the spirit man to supercede the physical man?? How do we conquer the physical minds that hinders progression into limitless potential? How do we conquer the eneMe once and for all?

How did I make the declaration that you can call me Victory?? Due to my having encountered several trials, frustrations and problems during the course of my life, and staying connected to God thru them all, I'm able to declare that I have been victorious. My beginnings were not grandiose beginnings. I was born to a single mom household in a local housing project with very minimal input from my earthly father. God didn't opt for my life to be that of those that have the privilege of being born in the suburbs, with a mother and father, a dog or a white picket fence. He desired that my life take an alternative path that I didn't understand or even like at the time but that later in life would be a life used to give others hope for a brighter and better tomorrow. He desired that my story be for his glory and now that I understand this, I appreciate having been chosen and simply thank God for finding me worthy enough to use and for trusting me with such an assignment.

My life in fact mimicked that of the butterfly. As we all know butterflies don't start out being that of the beautiful butterfly we see, however it starts as a not so pretty caterpillar. The caterpillar then endures the process of metamorphosis in which it enters into a cocoon. It's in the cocoon where the true struggle begins to get the caterpillar to its ultimate transformation—to that of a butterfly. It's told that the caterpillar struggles and fights in the cocoon to lose it's original look and gain its wings however if released to early will not form it's wings properly and therefore will never fly. So in order to soar it has to endure the grueling process and upon completion of the metamorphosis process, you will see a beautiful butterfly. So is the same in life, we will surely encounter grueling processes that we must go thru in order to get to the next levels in our lives. If we elude the process prematurely, we'll never be prepared to transition to the next level in life. The Bible teaches us that trials come to make us strong and the more trials, the stronger you are (so I must be the world's strongest woman☺). Too often when we're going thru trials we pray that God will deliver us instead of seeking God to determine what he's trying to teach us. At that rate you escape never learning the lesson and therefore you're bound to repeat this trial again.

Many times the eneME comes in when we continue to remember and remind ourselves of past failures, mistakes and mishaps. Quite often we live in the past which hinders progression into the future. One of my biggest hurdles was to overcome my past and family experiences. I always viewed myself as lil ol Nette from the project and thought I couldn't do anything big because I didn't know where to start. No one in my family had done anything I was trying to do (graduated college, owned a business, etc.). With that being a fact it became obvious to me that I wouldn't be able to do what I desired to do because of the self-imposed restrictions I placed on myself. I'd assumed the identity of a failure without making an honest attempt!! How often do we do this???

WRITING THE VISION

Studies have shown that when we write things down it goes into the subconscious mind. One time I read an article that stated in order to discover one's purpose in life you must write on a sheet of paper everything you enjoy and desire doing. Make a list of about 100 things and do a review and that which is repeated the most is your passion (that which you are designed to do). I challenged myself to do so and that which was repeated the most was in some way referencing helping people especially youth and women and funny because that's what I was doing as a Mental Health Counselor and with my non-profit organization. I discovered that my purpose and passion was one in the same but it all started with me writing the vision and making it plain but in that writing it became plain for me to see and discover what my purpose actually was and is.

Discovering your purpose

I've had several seasons in my life where I lost touch of the true me, the one you can't see—my spirit and was more in tune to the flesh which as we know in the flesh is no good thing and it can be somewhat confining. The flesh can at times be a distraction and used to hinder progression into purpose. We are taught in order to walk in the fullness of God we must "Die Daily" which is not a literal death where you actually die and are funeralized, but that you're killing the desires of the flesh to be closer to God. This closer walk with God helps one to realize their true purpose in God and the ability to walk in it.

Part of my dying process I had to forsake the desires of my flesh which was to abide by the pleasure principle or as we say in New Orleans Laissez les non temps rouler (let's let the good times roll)!! I took a vow of celibacy and made a pact with God to refrain from Sexual Intercourse until such time I was reunited in marriage. I did so in order to gain a closer relationship with God, discover some things about myself, do that which God had created me to do which is to be a blessing to others and ultimately discover the me that God sees. This process though was not an easy process, was indeed worthwhile. There were several occasions where my flesh began to rise and I wanted to take the deal off the table but God made me stick to my vow. On one occasion, I'd met a guy that was great to my kids and myself, very giving, kind hearted and was an overall blessing to my family (I thought) however he wasn't quite feeling the vow. I considered compromising the vow and just seek God's forgiveness for what I was contemplating on doing. On the day I'd made up my mind to go thru with the act, my cycle began that morning and this fella broke off our relationship that afternoon stating he was just going to go back to an ex of his yet we could remain friends. I couldn't be hurt (though I was and shocked to say the least) I could only laugh saying God you really have a sense of humor but I thank you for saving me from myself. This was a huge sacrifice for me because not only was I not in any consistent relationships mainly due to the vow but did not have a clue if or when I would actually be getting remarried. I'd met several guys along the way and when I would mention that I was celibate and the vow, many just threw their hands up instantly and others stuck around convincing themselves that I'd eventually change my mind. Besides the one previous time, I'd not thought of changing my mind because God caused me to see the vow as a commitment to him and that breaking it was like a breach of contract or simply put “lying to God.” I’d done enough being disobedient and lying to God and decided I’d try another approach didn’t want to keep trying the same thing expecting different results.

My mind would say, oh God will forgive you he forgives for everything and you’ll never get a boyfriend like that cause ain’t no man gon’ stick around not getting any!! My body would say this one time ain’t gon hurt not like you haven’t done it before. I had my mind and body opposing what my spirit knew was the right thing to do. Even one of my close friends suggested that I not tell guys I was celibate at the beginning because that runs people away and it’s too much to handle initially. I told her it’s supposed to run away those that are not a part of the purpose so in all actuality it’s doing just what it set out to do!! When we realize we don’t have a monopoly on God and that he moves as he pleases then he does just that “moves as he sees fit”. God allowed someone to return from my past, my first love to return to my life and after a short period of dating and getting to know each other again, he’s now my husband. This was a miracle in itself because I'd always been one to say "an ex is an ex for a reason" and that I'd never go back to someone that was a part of my past. I also said at the end of my first marriage and right before my divorce party, I'll never get married again" so now I see why the old folks would say "never say never" . . . lolol. This gentleman accepted the vow and my pact with God and also respected my request until we were married. In order for me to see myself as God sees me it took me to see myself as worthy to be waited for, worthy of God blessing me with someone that would respect that and capable of living a life that ultimately pleases him just as long as I am a willing vessel.

CHAPTER 5

When Losing is Winning

Indeed, I count everything as loss because of the surpassing worth of knowing Christ Jesus my Lord. For his sake, I have suffered the loss of all things and count them as rubbish, in order that I may gain Christ. Philippians 3:8

Destiny Manifested

I won I won I shot that BB gun, You lost, you lost you ate that applesauce was something we would chant as kids when a game or race of some sort was won (I guess I'm telling my age). As kids our ultimate goal in anything is to win because we are taught that losing is a bad thing. What's sad is that we grow into this same mentality that losing makes us a loser. In the Olympics, I sometimes enjoy watching the races just to see who's the fastest. When I see the winner of the Gold, I just think yeah that person was the fastest when in fact that may not have necessarily been the case. Although the grueling training process of much hard work, training daily sometimes 2-3 times a day and never giving up plays a major role, after doing some research, I learned it's not about being the fastest which helps one to win a race but being the smartest runner. You may be asking "what does intelligence have to do with winning a race?" Well I'll share with you what I learned which is closely paralleled with the Bible's teachings that the race is not necessarily given to the swift!! There was a write-up on how a race is won and the writer describes the winner of a race as one that knows when to make a move, is able to run their own race and finally the one that finds his/her fire!! It tells that the person that starts out with the leading crowd, should maintain their position in that crowd not falling behind or allowing themselves to be boxed in or left out. Next, to not get caught behind anyone that is slow but to focus on running your race, starting out and finishing in the front. Lastly, though the process has been both physically and mentally painful, to set your sights on something that gives you the desire to win (mom, children or self) and to keep the ammunition for winning in the back of your mind bringing it forth when you need it, in time to cross the finish line. So in a nutshell one that can keep their pace, run their race without concerning themselves with the race of the competitors (or living the life of someone else because of envy) and in the end pull themselves ahead of the gang, is the winner. How eerily similar is it in this race of life for those that WIN or succeed in life!!! We must be able to push pass fears of our past and the inner adversary that shouts to us that we won't win the race due to incompetence, lack of knowledge, resources and abilities and set realistic goals for our lives that will enable us to silence the voice of the ene-ME!!!

WIN OR LOSE OR LOSE AND WIN!!

One day a question was posed, do you want to win or lose? I thought on that for a moment because I as do many of us do enjoy winning. Well in my journey thru this life and as I've gotten older, I've realized winning the battle is not as important as winning the war which simply means that there will be some losses along the way to "Ultimate Victory" so in some cases losing is winning. I know you're asking how is that possible! I still enjoy winning however what I realized is that losing has taught me some valuable lessons and that in many of my losses I've gained so I still won!! I know that sounds strange and you're asking "How can you win if you lose?" . . . . well let me give you an example of what I mean. The most horrific year of my life was 2005. My family and I endured some of the greatest losses I can fathom. My mom's oldest and youngest brothers (my 2 favorite uncles) died 3 months apart, one died in March and the other in June, and these were her closest siblings, my 12 year old cousin killed herself in April and to top that year off we endured the most horrific Hurricane in the history of the United States, Hurricane Katrina. We loss everything, the house and all of our worldly possessions that were in it and when I say all I mean ALLLLLLL. My life prior to August 29, 2005 was totally erased and at this point is a mere memory because I had nothing tangible to prove an existence prior to that day. Indeed the experience was traumatic and I actually was not sure I'd make it through that year, in fact many days I didn't even have a desire to go on. In spite of all we went thru, God saw it, he heard my daily sometimes hourly cries and rewarded my family openly and publicly as a result of my private cries and prayers. God allowed us to gain double as a result of that loss and allowed us to see a flourishing end. Upon completion of the process God had my family and I to endure, we had a totally renovated house, all new furniture and had enough to pay off a 30 year home loan in 10 years. Thru that process of losing, I was rewarded given double of what was loss and gained a deeper relationship with God and more faith than I'd ever had before so I'd say thou it was a losing situation, I won.

Another loss was as recent as last year. I was employed at a Mental Health Rehabilitation Agency as a Program Manager. One day we were called into a meeting to announce the CEO's decision of closing the agency. We were given a 60-days notice and in his words was ample enough time for employees to find other employment and for me as the Program Manager to successfully transition clients to another agency for service. Well, within 2 weeks of the meeting, he shut the doors—I was out of a job. As you may be aware, at that time I was a single mother of 2 and both attend private schools. Due to not having ample time to find other employment, I applied for food stamps and unemployment. I was told by the Food Stamp Office that my income for the previous month was too much, that I'd have to wait another month to apply and told by unemployment that it was taking up to 10 weeks to process claims. So God, how am I supposed to survive on $300.00 a month when I have tuition of approximately $800.00 a month, car note almost $600.00 a month (I had a Lexus at the time y'all☺), car insurance approximately $230.00, and other household expenses (cell phone, lights, water, etc.). I prayed night, morning, midday, breakfast, lunch, snacktime and dinnertime because I knew only God could do this one. To add insult to injury, my kids and I were returning home from church the Sunday morning, September 12, 2010 to be exact after my last day on the job and a guy ran the stop sign and totaled my car. So now I've loss my car and income what did that mean for me? Well it meant I had to trust

God like never before and I did. The kind gentleman that totaled my car also didn't have insurance but like a good neighbor, you know who was there . . . (my insurance company)!!! They not only paid my totaled vehicle out, but gave me a check for almost $8,000.00 which was enough to purchase another vehicle and live off until I gained another job. I loss but I won again!!! After that blessing, a week later I finally received my unemployment debit card which had in excess of $1,000 on it and a refund check from Lexus Financial services because the payoff check sent by my Insurance Company exceeded the amount that was due. Can you say . . . . WINNING!!!!!!!

As you read further along, I will talk about how losing though sometimes seems like failure and can really hurt, it's sometimes for our good. Sometimes losing makes the transition to winning a lot easier.

3, 2, 1 . . . . Takeoff !!!

One day I was in my Zumba class and at the end of the workout, we were in the cooling down process. The instructor had us doing shoulder rolls—roll them back now roll them forward is what she said. The young lady that stood next to me proclaimed "it hurts to move forward." At that time the instructor and I looked at each other and said "wow, how prophetic was that" because I'd been coaching the instructor through life for several months at this time. The way I was able to coach the instructor is because I'd already been there. You know where there is—the place of complacency and comfort that you're afraid to leave until God makes your comfort zone uncomfortable—that place.

Many times we affiliate the lack of moving forward as fear of progression which is true to an extent. We are afraid to go where we've never gone. As for me, I have a controlling personality which allows me to know and facilitate how things go in my life because I'm the captain of my faith (is what I used to foolishly tell myself) so going into what I didn't know—that transition was always uncomfortable to me because I felt as if I was not going to be in control because

I didn't know. Well what I realized it was not fear alone, but it hurt to move forward because with every form of progression, there's some regression. We lose a lot to move forward which is the painful part. We lose some friends and family, we have to leave some things behind and sometimes we lose ourselves. What I've learned over the years is losing of the excess only makes the climb to the top a lot easier besides everything and everyone is not designed for your next level. Just call it your preparation for takeoff or take-off!!

I can recall the last time the space shuttle took off and a friend and I had lunch that day. We got into a conversation regarding the takeoff and was able to see how God can bring forth a revelation as a result of a Space shuttle take off. After doing a little research again, I learned that at the time of takeoff for the shuttle, it consists of the "stack" which includes a dark orange-colored external tank, two white, slender Solid Rocket Boosters (SRB); and the component that contains the crew and payload which is referred to as the Orbiter Vehicle. Some payloads were launched into higher orbits with either of two different booster stages developed for the STS. The Space Shuttle was then stacked and the stack mounted on a mobile launch platform held down by four explosive bolts on each SRB which are detonated at the time of the launch.

The shuttle stack launched vertically like a conventional rocket. It lifted off under the power of its two SRBs and three main engines, which were fueled by liquid hydrogen and liquid oxygen from the external tank. The Space Shuttle had a two-stage ascent. The SRBs provided additional thrust during liftoff and first-stage flight. About two minutes after liftoff, explosive bolts were fired, releasing the SRBs, which then parachuted into the ocean, to be retrieved by ships for refurbishment and reuse. Do you see God yet?? Let me help you, the shuttle is in tact when it initially takes off with all the excess weight and parts as they are necessary to get it to a certain point however in order to reach its full altitude it has to shed the excess weight . . . it had to lose all the extras in order to gain altitude and get to its' highest point or reach its full potential. The shuttle has to shed its SRBs and drop them into the ocean to go higher. What are the SRBs (spirit of ridicule and badgering) you have to shed in order to reach your full altitude/potential??

Our lives mimic that of a tree. We know how trees will lose all their leaves during the transition of seasons.

During one season it blossoms and has all of its leaves however when there's a change in seasons it losses all of its leaves but the loss of leaves does not dictate the death of the tree as much as it indicates the change in seasons and how it's being prepared to endure until it's time comes again to flourish. If we parallel this transition to our lives we can clearly see how during certain seasons of our lives, God strips us of our leaves (bad habits, people, self-destructing behaviors, etc.) in order to prepare us for the next season of life. Once the negative has been taken off by us, by God, etc. we can then accentuate the positives and walk into purpose!!

CHAPTER 6

Walking Into Your Purpose

The steps of a good man are ordered by the Lord, and he delights in his way. Though he fall, he shall not be utterly cast down; for the Lord uphold him with his hand. Psalm 37:23-24

LADIES WE KNOW when we're dating someone and it gets to a certain level of seriousness we start looking to going to the next level which is some cases is a Promise Ring which precedes the engagement ring. The promise ring is indicative that there's a level of commitment that will at some point in the future lead to an engagement and later to a marriage. Many women rejoice over the promise of marriage without having a date for engagement let alone a wedding date. We start preparing, going to bridal shows, trying on gowns, thinking of colors and guest list . . . the whole nine. We just praise on the promise. Let's think if we transferred that level of intensity into preparing and praising on the promises of God how much more of a success we would be. When God provides a revelation for something that will later manifest in our lives, we should start planning as if the date has been etched in stone. If it's the vision of your own business someday, with the promise you rush out to name your business, then work on the business plan, then look for the building, work on a budget or if God promises you will have a college degree, you rush out start filling out college applications, apply for financial aid, put monies on the side for books, buy school supplies, etc.

Praising on the promise is merely putting your faith to work and convincing your heart and mind to believe that which your spirit already knows. When we praise on the promise, it's like laughing in the face of the eneMe saying I know what you're saying but I'll step out on faith because I know that God knows what's best for my life. God if you said it and took the time to reveal it to me, than I believe it. However, too often, we not only wait to praise until the promise is a present. Sometimes we give up before the vision comes to fruition thinking we were dreaming and it wasn't a vision from God. Are you convincing yourself that you are not worthy of the blessings of God or that he is a God that can't do what he said or he's just a liar. Well let me share this with you, God can and will do all that he promised and more than you can imagine. You think small business, he's able to provide you a chain of businesses, you think nice house God's able to provide a mansion on a hill, you think Toyota in the driveway, he can provide a Lexus in a garage. We must stop tying God's hands and be specific but be big. When God reveals things to me and my eneME begins to tell me I was hallucinating, I start over talking him by talking to God. I say: "God you said that the cattle on a thousand hills are yours and that I can have what I ask if I ask, that if I paid my tithes which I do that you would open the windows of heaven and pour me out a blessing that I won't have room enough to receive. Well God I have a bunch of room right now so what's up?? God it's impossible for you to lie and with you it's impossible for me to fail so I need you to make this here situation right because it's not for man to believe me, I told them what you said so they're gonna doubt you and I know you won't let that happen, so come on by here my Lord, In Jesus name I pray. Amen"!! God moves when you speak with authority because he can't lie so he will come and honor his word to you but the question is will you move when he tells you to and honor the purpose he's instilled in you?

GETTING PASS YOUR PAST

As I sit on my bed, confused, frustrated and just plain ol' exhausted with life. I told my husband at that time that I needed a divorce. For the sake of my sanity, he had to go and so did I. I was in a stressful job and to come to a stressful home everyday had me totally out of sync, I had no peace anywhere and something had to be done. So divorce it is but how did we get here and have only been married 5 years. At this point I went on what I called a Quest for Me. I had to figure out the part I played in the demise of my marriage because my beliefs are that it takes 2 to either make a relationship work or to destroy a relationship, so what role did I play.

As I began my reflections, I began to realize from the very beginning of my marriage I saw an expiration date which means it was doomed before it began. But how was it that I declared it over from the start? Where did that come from? As I reflected all the more I discovered something that I thought I'd overcome years before-my daddy issues. As I've previously stated, my dad and I had a sketchy relationship to start but later became non-existent but the problem was he was the first man in my life that I very well should have been able to rely on and he wasn't so he gave men a bad name in my mind and therefore no man would ever stand a chance with me because I viewed them all as unreliable. I never realized how I treated men or better yet my husband until I began that reflection and the root of the problem. My past had become my present but as I went on became my future until I was able to disconnect totally and get past my past. How is this done? Can this be done overnight? How does one get pass their past?

In so many ways we struggle with getting pass our past because of the bad experiences (break ups, deaths, regrets, bad relationships, etc.) not reflecting on the good experiences and how ultimately the past has assisted in forming us. My past even though it was behind me, quite often I would drag it into my present. Charles Kettering says You can't have a better tomorrow if you are thinking about yesterday all the time. The mind only knows the past and will quite often use it against you to prohibit your progression into success telling you things like "You failed the first time you tried it so you're probably going to fail again". The past should be viewed more like a blueprint to learn from. I did this last time and it didn't work so let me try another way. Past failures should be used as learning experiences and not future failure indicators. When we know better it should assist us with doing better.

In order to get pass my past, I had to address the experiences which was not done by covering them up but addressing them head on and no longer allowing them to control me and be a hindrance to progression.

Stop Talking, Just Do IT!!

Just Do It, was a 3 word phrase made famous in 1988 by a famous shoe company. The phrase was coined at a meeting with the company's ad agency and was used to inform everyone of the company's can-do attitude. This came about at a time when the company was not at all in a winning position yet when they were trailing behind another famous shoe company. The company was actually trailing behind their competitors, the Reebok shoe company and was compelled to come up with something that would pulling past their competition and securing the number 1 spot in this industry. This caused them to speak their destiny into existence as they came up with a tactic that has allowed them to be superior in their market ever since. "Just Do It", just did it for them. The phrase alone spoke to the passion and determination of people which made people feel empowered and compelled to wear their tennis shoes and the T-shirts that possessed the phrase. A mere 3 word phrase caused the company to grow, expand and succeed at a drastic and swift rate. Over a span of 10 years, they went from \$877 million in sales to \$9.2 billion. What they said, "Just do it", persuaded them to do what it took to succeed and encouraged them enough to persevere.

I'd come to a crossroad as it regarded my non-organization after I'd been dormant for more than a year I struggled with whether to restart programming or to just shut it down. When I consulted with God he forbad me to shut it down, yet he gave me another opportunity however at this time I'd developed a better relationship with him and with his help was better equipped to silence the ene-ME. The problem with talking too much is that you can talk yourself out of opportunities before you have a chance to make it manifest. I knew what God had ordained me to do as it regarded my organization, however my eneME gave me every excuse as to why I shouldn't and that it couldn't be meant for this time (not enough money, not enough employees, overwhelming, etc.). The year I restarted, God gave me three events to conduct that would honor our commitment of helping people in the City of New Orleans and so that community is aware that we were resuming programming. One event was October, November and December. I was like wow God how do you expect me to do all of this and it was as if he responded by saying "Just do it". He reassured me that I didn't need the money or anything else just to be obedient and do it so I did. All 3 events were a success and that improved my faith and so my organization had resumed. To follow that year we began to do so many more things from events, to our first summer camp, to receiving our 501c3 non-profit status, to receiving grants, providing more services. We'd expanded rapidly and drastically but on top of all that, we were presented with another opportunity to expand even further and to do some other things in addition to our Summer Camp for the summer. As I read the requirements, the voices immediately started speaking you don't have the money to do this, you've never done this before, you're broke and this takes money to do this and something leaped in my spirit saying get up, fill out the application and send it right now. I was obedient to the spirit and I hurried filled out the application and faxed it before my eneME could talk me out of it. Upon faxing it, the voices were silenced. After that God began to open several doors to us so that we can be successful at this venture.

Many instances in life especially if we know it's something that we are supposed to do, in order to silence the voice of your inner enemy and so that it doesn't talk you out of opportunity, you must hush your enemy and by just doing it. The more time you allow to lapse, the more the voice will convince you not to do it, giving all type of fear responses that will scare you enough to walk away from something you should be walking into.

Your Mountaintop Moment

Many are the afflictions of the righteous; but the Lord delivereth him out of them all. Psalm 34:18-19. When referencing a mountain we think of something hard and in some cases seeming impossible to conquer. There are several references to mountains that we speak of as Christians and we use the mountain to represent troubles and difficulties. If I say to this mountain be thou removed or be thou cast into the sea, Lord give me the strength to climb this mountain or the song of old move mountain get out of my way—we talk about mountains rather often. Mountains simply represent difficulties and trials that we encounter in life and you may wonder why difficulties present themselves. Well the bible teaches us that trials (difficulties) come to make us strong and they have a distinct purpose in life. If you'd never had a problem then you wouldn't know that God can solve it or recognize the strength God's given us to endure.

Sometimes difficulties present themselves to humble us, to renew our faith in the Almighty, to help us to realize we're not in control, to realize our true purpose in life, etc. We must remember God said in his word that all things work together for good for those that love him which says the good and the bad collectively has a purpose that is ultimately good for us. I am a product of a single mother household, I was born and raised in poverty in a local housing project for the first 23 years of my life, I had little to no input in my life from my earthly father, I later in life became a single mother, I was single in a marriage, later divorced and then a single mother of not 1 but 2 children, unemployed, financial struggles, man troubles, I've had so many excuses I could've used in order to excuse myself from succeeding. Yet all the good not only outweighed the bad but all the experiences helped to form me into the person that I am today. In a nutshell, I wouldn't have a testimony, had I not had a test!

I read an article that said "Children that are products of single-parent families are faced with a number of academic risk factors and are three times more likely to drop out of high school than children who live with both parents, even when they have the same intelligence levels and academic capabilities. Also that many teens who live in single-parent households with high poverty rates become teen parents and were five times as likely to be poor as children in households where both parents were present. The combination of poverty and single parenthood negatively affects a child's academic progress. There is often more parental distress and less supervision in the home. A study by the National Center for Education and Statistics followed the academic progress of children who were classified as "at-risk" for academic failure (children from single-parent households, children whose mothers had not completed high school, and children whose mothers were on public assistance). These children consistently had lower test scores in math, reading and science. OOOh I was counted out before I could get started and this could've been my excuse to fail in life. My mother was a single mother and we lived on public assistance however the destiny that man determined for me was not the same that God ordained for me. In spite of my pre-determined destiny, circumstances in life, my being a single parent, etc. I never had issues academically and though I did not like science I didn't fail a science course until College somewhere according to society I wasn't supposed to be being the product of a single mother household and all!! Yet today I am a 1st generation college graduate possessing a Bachelor and Masters Degree (yep lil Nette from the project), am happily married (better the

2nd time around), a owner of not 1 but 2 businesses, a motivational speaker and much more.

I think the obstacles in life got me to this point because I wouldn't be able to tell the kids I work with that where you start in life doesn't determine where you go if I hadn't had the start I had. Nor would I be able to tell them that excuses are used for failure. I share my story with women, youth, men and anyone I feel can use a ray of hope. It's not for the sake of telling my business because those that know me closely know how uncomfortable it is for me to be transparent but I had to realize my story is ultimately for God's glory. I'm more comfortable speaking of every mountain God's brought me over, every trial he's seen me thru yet for every blessing I say hallelujah and for all things I give him praise. I see the bad as my learning experiences and preparation for the good that is to come. In my bad times I'm afforded an opportunity to see God in another element, in need I see him as Jehovah Jireh (my provider), when I struggle mentally and circumstances have me confused I see him as Jehovah Shalom (my peace) and when in the fight of my life El-Shaddai (God of the mountains or God Almighty).

What obstacles have you encountered in life that you can use to catapult you into your purpose? What opportunities have you allowed the EneMe to convince you, that you were too inadequate to do? Will you continue to allow the Ene-Me to deprive you of the luxuries associated with you walking into your purpose? Just know in order to delight in your Mountain top experience you must first silence the voice of your eneMe (faith cancels fear), know that you can do all things thru Christ because he strengthens you and at the end of the day to get to the top of the mountain, you have to climb it. That means some struggles, some bumps and bruises, shedding some excess pounds, encouraging yourself that you can do it even when your body and mind is working against you, etc. The Mountain top experience makes the struggle worth it!!!

Closing Remarks

CONQUERING THE ENEME is indeed an ongoing process that has to be done on a consistent basis. There will always be scenarios in life when the little voice of the inside arises and the process has to be implemented again. The EneMe will be present and with you until you die. My Bishop taught us that there will always be a certain level of fear we'll encounter especially when being called to another level in our lives but how we handle these situations will determine whether we fail or succeed in life. The objective of the book is not to give you the illusion that this is a one-time battle, but to make you aware that it is an ongoing process, help you with identifying, addressing and silencing the voice and the necessary steps to conquer it each time it arises. Though I've come far in life, my eneME still comes to attack and many times in a way that it has come before but because the word declares that I am more than a conqueror I know that I can conquer the Enemy that speaks against my destiny even when it's me!! You can't get mad at the enemy for doing its job, but it should motivate us to do ours which is to succeed on purpose in spite of adversities.

www.ingramcontent.com/pod-product-compliance
Ingram Content Group UK Ltd.
Pitfield, Milton Keynes, MK11 3LW, UK
UKHW041933190726
13854UKWH00004B/1574